When Love Glows

Victor Akinrinmade

authorHOUSE®

AuthorHouse™
1663 Liberty Drive
Bloomington, IN 47403
www.authorhouse.com
Phone: 1-800-839-8640

Published by AuthorHouse 3/8/2012

ISBN: 978-1-4685-6122-7 (e)
ISBN: 978-1-4685-6005-3 (sc)

Library of Congress Control Number: 2012904221

Table of Contents

How Wonderful It Looks

It is a lovely day
my lovely;
you look so bright
today my dear.

Make it your day;
make it a day;
the morning of joy
to you, my love.

How wonderful it looks
to me my love;
it is so bright, and
you glow with it.

Give me a smile,
my love I plea;
for a smile from
you will make a
day.

When the Part Seems Rough

It is so rough you said
my love;
how could the promise
come to stay.

You wonder through
the land and sea;
oh tell me when
it will come to
stay.

But I tell you my
love so dear, that
love will win
at last my dear.

The part so rough
today my love,
will pave the way
for days to come.

How wonderland
will become my love?

It will come to stay
in time to come.

Victor Akinrinmade

You Remind Me of the Day We Met

You remind me of
everything;
the day I first met
you my love.

Your beautiful eyes;
your beautiful smile;
and a body to go
with it.

I'm grateful dear
that I meet you
so;
because you come with
joy and love.

How I need you;
how I love you;
from that day on,
I know you're right.

What a beauty;
what a great joy
you bring into my life
my love.

You haven't change
all this time my
love;
you remind me of
the day we
met.

Victor Akinrinmade

It's Coming Soon My Love

I've got a parcel full
of love;
for you my love,
for you.

My parcel is my
love for you,
and who can tell
the end of it?

It's coming soon,
my love for you,
as I move on
to post it through.

This parcel dear is
the best I've got;

and I tell you, you
will love it too.

Who can know it?

Who can break it?

Because my love is
stronger than death.

Expect it soon;
it won't be long,
it's coming soon my
love for you.

Victor Akinrinmade

The Market Place of Love

Your smile betrays your
beauty love, as I
search the market
place of love.

I went to the
market place my
dear;
searching and searching
for the one for
me.

My shoes wear out,
I feel worn out,
then I saw your
smiling face.

Your beautiful glow
like a brilliant
star;
I see you come my
way my love.

You cooled my thirst,
you refreshed my
soul;
all in the market
place of love.

The Mirror of My Soul

You are a mirror of
my soul my love;
you make me smile,
you make me cry,
you make me rejoice
in the days to come.

You're so lovely dear;
you are so good;
you bring a joy
to my soul my
love.

The thinking of you
makes me smile
again;
and the thinking
of you makes me
cry for you.

My soul but knows
I love you so,
as my soul but
love you too.

Victor Akinrinmade

For The Love I Know

It is a good thought
to know your love,
as I write for the
love I know.

Who would tell
me you but
exist?

But seeing you,
my dreams comes
true.

As I move on I
wonder dear;
who would but tell
my love?

Thinking of you;
dreaming of you;
as I but write for
the love I know.

The Source of the Wind

What is the source of
the wind my love?

It whispers love,
it whispers joy,
it tells me sure,
the love is true.

The source of the wind
is love I heard,
as the wind but
whistles on and
on.

What is the source
of joy my love?

It whispers love;
it whispers peace;
the source of joy
is love I heard.

So my dear love,
you got to know
that the bond of
love is strong my
dear.

It's Time for My Love to Rise

When I see the sun
rising up my dear,
I say it's done;
my joy is come.

When I see the moon
come up in night,
I say it's done;
my peace is come.

But seeing you come
my way my love;
I know my love is
come my way.

How I love you;
how I need you;
the time have come
for me to love.

Oh loving you;
oh needing you;
is one thing dear,
I won't regret.

The Breaking of the Dawn

I see the breaking
dawn my love,
and the rising sun
my dear.

It's time for love to
wake my dear, and
joy with it my
love.

Who would but think
that you will be
mine?

The sun told me
and too.

The breaking dawn
of love is come,
and I know the
joy is mine.

Who would but think
the sun would rise
after the darkness
oh my love?

Oh my love, I'm
glad it rise at the
breaking of the dawn,
my love.

Victor Akinrinmade

When the Going Is Good

I can guess my love,
I can; that hope
seems gone will come
anew.

Tell me the truth;
tell me my love;
can the hope gone
become anew?

This thing I know
and get refreshed;
when the going is
good my love.

Where would you go
from here my
love?

I know the going is
good my love.

Think it today,
think it my love,
and joy will come
our way my love.

My Lake Is On the Desert Land

The only lake in my
desert land is you,
my love is you.

With coconut trees
surrounding you;
my lake is clear
as a crystal sea,
and I love you,
my love I do.

The source of my lake
is you my dear,
and it flows and
on and on my
love.

My lake is the best
my desert is got,
and because of it,
my desert but
glows.

Who won't but smile,
who won't but come
to see my desert
turn a green
land.

Victor Akinrinmade

The Leaves Remind of You

I see the leaves dropping
from the tree and
I wonder why they
do.

But they tell me in
voice so sad, they
need you so they
said.

From the day you stop
coming to the
tree, the leaves
begins to drop.

If leaves reminds
of you my love,
what would I do
my dear?

I love you more
than leaves my dear,
and I need you
every day and more.

The tree could not
bear its lose my
love;
I can't believe all
the leaves drops off.

The leaves reminds
of you my love.

Writing You a Love Letter

How are you my love
I said;
why do you shine
with love my dear?
I want to know
how you do it.

You shine but on
and on my love;
how heaven knows I
love you so;
they say I love
too much my love.

I'm writing you a
love letter,
for this will bring
the news to you.

Seating by Myself

Oh my love, I'm
thinking of you;
I seat alone by
myself my love.

Thinking of you every
day of my life will
bring great joy,
will bring great
love.

I'm thinking of you
my love;
talking of you
my love,
my joy.

I talk of you
every day of my life,
who won't but think
of you my love?
I can't regret
my love for you.

Victor Akinrinmade

The Rainbow in the Sky

I see your rainbow
Through my sky;
My love I really do.

Who would but say it
can be you?

My love you are
too good to me.

The rainbow in the
sky comes through
my love and I
can't believe my
eyes.

It shows your beauty
from head to
toe;
and you're a one
of love.

The rainbow in the
sky so clear
brings you to me
in days to
come.

Hand in Hand

I feel the breeze
blowing in my hair,
as my legs move
to and fro the
beach.

Who would but
wonders what goes
on,
as the rainbow in
the sky makes a
crown for me.

I splash my feet
in the water dear,
and I know I love
you so my dear.

As we move about
hand in hand my love;
I feel the current flows
through me.

How I love you;
how I need you;
you know the flowers
love the bee
my love.

As the water falls
my love,
my dear,
the beauty of it
not compared to
yours.

I Will Meet You

I will my love
the same my dear,
I will meet you at
the point of love.

Many wonders;
many want it;
but the point of
love is the one
for us.

When you love me
the way you do,
as I love you the
way I do.

The point of love
is the meeting
love.

I will meet you
at the point of
love.

A Beauty That Falls

I rush to hold you
when you fall;
what makes a love
like you to fall?

A beauty that falls
is picked at once;
and you're no
exception my love;
my dear.

What makes you fall
in love my dear?

A beauty like you
is meant to stand.

But thanks oh dear
that you do fall,
or what would have
been my chance
my dear.

I've seen so many
day my love;
but the best of it
is falling in
love.

Your Water Flows

Like a spring you are
to me my love;
your water flows from
shore to shore.

Out of nowhere you
spring anew;
your water sooths
my soul my love.

Your spring of love;
your spring of joy;
I love to drink
it more and more.

Your love just flows
along my part, and
call me so with voice
so sweet.

I move so fast to
suck your love;
and swim in the
spring that glows
with love.

Your water flows
from shore to
shore.

The Taste of Your Lips

The curve of your lips
makes me yearn
for you
oh my love,
I need you so.

Your beautiful hair sings
a loving song;
and your beautiful eyes
tells me all of
love.

But I don't want
to go too low;
but your beautiful
breast reminds me
of my need.

I won't go lower
than this my love,
but your lips are
making me yearn
my love.

Oh mine, my love,
your voice so dear:
as the taste of
your lips makes
me need you
more.

The Beauty from Within

You're so beautiful
my love;
even the heaven
knows it too.

I hear the sky scream
love for you;
I hear the joy of
Love for me.

Thinking of you
will make the joy;
a beauty from within
is you my love.

I refuse to give
up my dear, as you
keep on laughing
on my love.

You're beautiful;
as I dream of you
my love.

Roses Are Red

I see rose glow
red my love, and
I remember my love
for you.

The thinking of you,
my love for you,
brings tears into my
eyes, my love.

Who won't remember
you my love;
a beauty that but
comes alive.

The rose glows red;
your beauty glows bright;
you're better than
rose my love.

How great it is to know
you dear;
you make me glow
from within my love.

It is a Crime Not to Love You

You won't believe it,
my love,
my dear;
but it is a crime not
to love you.

You're just too good
with heart so
pure, and
why won't I but
loving you?

You are my love,
and I love you;
a regret I never
have.

My thought is right
as my mind is right,
and I decide to
stick to love.

I keep on loving
you my love;
as the future
will tell my
dear.

The Hope and Joy

When the rising sun
come down my way;
I rise and shine
like a star my
love.

You are my love;
you are my joy;
as I move on from
hand to hand.

The hope and joy
move hand in hand,
and I join too
my hand to yours.

Let's join with hope;
let's join with joy;
since hope and joy
make all our day.

As you but see my
loving one,
that joy is come to
stay.

The Old Man Said

I saw an old man
on the beach my love,
and he thinks, and
thinks of love my dear.

That love rejoice,
and he never know
when love gives up.

Thinking of love,
he said to me,
that the sun will
always show my
love.

To him love glows
like a star my love,
and love won't give
up hope my dear.

The old man said
in a whisper dear,
that love is won
the war my love.

Victor Akinrinmade

I Know That Love

Wondering when to see
you again, as love
seems gone to me
my love.

Hope will come anew
I said to me;
I wonder on and
on my dear.

Tell me the truth,
my love I said, as
hope seems gone
renews itself.

I know that love
renews itself, but
hope and joy must
mingle so.

Tell me the truth,
tell me my joy,
as you know that love
but speaks the truth.

I love you so, my
love I said;
as words but sings
their songs my
love.

I Remember the Day

To think of love
is what to do my
love;
a dream of love that
comes to stay.

I remember the day
my love grows
up.

She looks so bright,
she looks so nice
as love grows up
to show the
world.

Who won't wonder
what to think
my love.

When love but glows
the way she does,
a brilliant light
within a room;
who won't wonder
what to say my love?

As you decide to
show yourself.

My Heart Loves You

Who won't wonder
why you love me
so.

My heart yearns
so,
my heart loves
you,
a joy that
comes from joy
my love.

Thinking of you
my love I say,
a dream that
comes through all
my way;

my love I know
the truth is come
to stay the way
only love could
stay.

My love how much
I love you so;
you love you so;
you love me so,
I love you too as
love mingles with
love my dear.

The Bell of Love

The joy that loves
you more and more,
as love but rings
it's bell my dear.

When life but say
that love will,
you wonder how it
will my love.

Let us ring it;
the bell of love
as we ring and
the love to come.

I remember now,
my love, my dear,
that the love that
comes will come to
stay.

Oh my dear love,
oh my dear joy
as I look into
your eyes my
love.

Why it Flows

Did you see it, the
tears my love?

I can't imagine
It falls that way.

Why does a man cry
so my love?

But a tear of love
just drops that
way.

I cry for you my
love, my dear;
a joy that
mingles so my
love.

Who won't wonder
why it flows that
way?

The joy that comes
with love my
dear.

I've cried so many
tears my love,
because I love you
so my dear.

Who Won't Wonder

What a beautiful
eyes my love;
you look so bright
in the light
my love.

Who won't wonder
how you look my
love
as a brilliant light
in a glow my
love.

Oh tell me your
love;
oh tell me you
joy
as a lighten dear,
you struck my soul.

Many wonder how
you look so
bright;
but your beautiful
eyes instructs me
so.

Your Beautiful Hair

What a beautiful hair
you've got;
I love the way
you bind it dear.

Your posture speaks
of love my dear,
your brilliant smile
reminds of love.

You bend your head
in love my
dear,
as your speaking
love reminds
of you.

Make me so proud
with joy my love
unbound your hair,
and let it flow.

And what a beautiful
hair you've got my
love.

You Are a Joy to Know

Going round and round
the word would say
as I leaning on
the love I know.

I love you so, my
love I say as I
thinking of what
to say.

You're a joy to
know,
you're a joy to
think as a
loving on my
soul but say.

Thinking of you
my love I say,
the joy that brings
me joy and love.

You are Beautiful

How wonderful it is
to love you so;
you're brilliant love
from head to toe;
eying you through
my love I say,
as love do speak
of love my
dear.

You're beautiful
dear, my love,
my joy as I
yearn for you
all day my
love.

Wanting you so;
needing you so;
as I need you
all day my
love.

Your Pretty Legs

I see you moving
all around with
frame so good my love,
my dear.

Your pretty legs tell
me of love,
and your beautiful
hands tell me of
joy.

From head to toe,
you are beautiful
love;
how I love you
my heart but say.

To dream of love
is good my dear;
who won't dream
it as life goes on?

You're beautiful my
joy;
as you move around
my love.

It Glows of Love

Look at the flower
oh my love,
as it glows and glows
of love my dear.

It glows of life,
it glows of love,
it glows of peace
that comes with it.

Your flower tell
of my love for
you,
as a beauty of
yours just glows
like one.

You darling flower;
my love,
my dear,
as you tell me
of hope my
love.

My Love

I saw the eyes that
makes me cry,
the dawning cloud
that makes me
scream.

Oh my love, my
love I say,
the only heart that
fits my soul.

Oh you said it,
oh I know it,
but my love, you
know I love
you so.

Draining the rain that
clouds my eyes,
the tears that mingle
so my love.

My soul but cry,
my soul but scream,
the only heart my
soul but love.

The Breaking Tour

Pregnant with words
as the anger
unspoken eats
me out.

How can the glows
make dim so
dark?

The breaking tour
of my life so
bright.

I remember the
day so clear,
as bright as the sun
my love.

What makes the warm
so cold my love?

A future bright today
and gone?

I can but see,
I can but tell,
that love is as
strong as death.

The Turning Wheel

The love that goes
my part today will
spring the day to
me tonight.

How can it be?

How can you say?

That love so blind
that wakes me so.

The turning wheel
that rule the day
is the only thing
that makes my
day.

Love is the word;
love is the way,
and my heart but
yearns for it I
know.

Your Touch Breaks Me

Leave me alone;
leave me I say,
you know I tell
you so.

Your touch breaks
me;
your words melts
me;
I drawn in the
sea of love.

Don't touch me
dear;
don't look at me
dear,
you know I want
you so.

But like a dream
that fades away,
my soul instructs
me so.

Leave me alone;
leave me I say;
I hope you know
my love.

You Never Know

You wonder where
it comes from,
when a love you
never know, shows
a saving hand
from the blue.

I'm grateful dear;
I really do,
but I don't know
how to thank
you much.

Thinking and flowing
words would say,
that love alone
can make the
day.

You but said it;
you but know it,
without a word it's
know around.

Thank you I say;
thank you my love,
if only love would
say the word.

Think It My Love

I can see my way
come clear;
the willow just but
said it come.

Think it my love;
think it my dear,
that love and joy
that makes my
day.

What would the
wonder say my love?

What can the love
so great but yearn?

I can see you,
I can tell you,
a soul that makes
me yearn for you.

River of My Soul

Like a river flowing
in and out,
so the dream of
my life today;

tik...
tik...
tik...

the same the way
to me my love.

What would the poor
heart say my love?

You held the key,
and keep it safe;

tik...
tik...
tik...

so the river of my
soul but flows.

How I love you;
how I need you,
but like a stream
it flows away.

Victor Akinrinmade

You Know My Love

My day is come for
me to stay,
to tell my heart
his love is come.

Oh yes, the wonder
goes;
and love my heart
for me but say.

Why talk it so
loud my heart?

You know my
love loves the
peace of mind.

Don't talk too much;
don't talk too loud,
for whisper dear will
rhyme with love.

Oh yes I know;
oh yes you care;
your love for her
is one I know.

Do You Know

Oh my love,
my heart,
my joy;
do you know how
much I love
you so?

When last my love,
when last...
did I tell you
that I love
you so?

My dear;
my love;
my beauty in
joy
that makes my day
so bright.

Look at my eyes,
and what do you
see?

I guess you see
my love,
speaking its words
to you.

Listen my love,
the drum is low,
as joy and brightness
mingle so.

Your Beauty

It is the dawn of
a life my love;
the making it is
the word to say.

The bright and gloom,
the love and pain,
but love rewards
her own.

My love I can't
but say,
you shine like
moon in night.

Your beauty makes
my face but shine,
your smile makes
me forget my pain.

Oh dear my love;
oh dear my joy;
your beauty makes
it one and all.

Victor Akinrinmade

As Strong As Fire

What a couple?

What a pair?

And love the ring
that fix the
day.

In my few days
I'm yet to see
a love as
strong as fire.

With the love's
hand leading the
way;
I'm sure the future
Is bright.

A honeymoon on a
tree house my
love?

I Will Let You Know

Your is shaking
me like a tree.

You make me your
own my love
is all I ask
of you;
and I promise you
myself.

Let the world
know my love,
let the world
know,
a love you
make of me.

And I will
let her know
what a love you
are my love.

Victor Akinrinmade

Think My Love

She writes with a
golden ink;
a pen like a crystal
sea.

Have you met
her?

Have you seen
her?

The heart my soul
but loves.

She shines like a
glowing sun;
a heart like a
blending love;
oh yes, you must
but meet her
soon.

But think my love,
but think;
you must meet her
my love.

Oh Dear My Heart

Be patient my soul;
be patient my heart;
your love will come
your way, and soon.

Oh yes I know that
life is unkind,
but the truth is this
you will grow but
strong.

Oh dear, my heart;
oh dear, my soul;
don't give up now
for your goal is
near.

Your love seems
far away,
but you know she's
near.

You know it's
true.

I Keep My Day

The going is good,
the part is nice,
a bit, and down
it goes.

How can you say
the day is bright?
I can but see the
sun go sleep.

Oh dear my love;
oh dear my joy;
you just but said
I keep my day.

Don't say it now;
don't say it yet;
my heart but yearns,
my soul but waits.

Oh dear my love;
oh dear my joy;
you know I love
you so.

The Part of My Life

Telling the blue from
the string,
how can the wonder
of my life but
show?

You said that you
know my part,
the part of my
life that leads
to you.

Oh dear my love;
oh dear my own;
you know the
door is there for
you.

What makes you waste
your life away?

What makes you leave
your life behind?

My love,
my dear,
my hope,
my joy;
the wonder thing
my soul but loves.

Victor Akinrinmade

You But Said It

Never me betray my
soul;
the heart that wonders
so my love.

Oh think me go
the part my way
and wonder still the
part to go.

You but said it;
you but know it;
a wonder stick in
the bush I guess.

Never but wonder
much my love;
never but think
it dull my love.

You know that soul
that thinks and
shines,
is the soul that
will see another
day.

Who Will Tell Her

How can the world
know now?

Who would but tell
her now?

Please dream sweet
dream,
please talk sweet
talk,
as the world my love
will come to know.

Who would tell her?

Who would make it?

That my soul but
yearns for the one
I love.

I promise do;
I promise say;
but my promise for
my love but say.

She Comes My Way

I loss my love
to her;
the she that I
but loves.

What makes her so
strong and fair?

The thinking that
makes my day.

How would you say
it now?

What would you say
but love?

I know the day
she comes my way;
and what my love
but guess?

My happiness is making
guess,
but I love and love
her so.

Walk It Through Night

Like the arm so strong,
like the heart so great,
and she comes to me
at last.

Oh great the day
I see it come,
and love the word to
say.

Walk it through night,
walk it through day,
but my love will
make my day.

Take it my love,
take it my day,
she will do it but
now and then.

Oh my…
oh my…
but my love but
smiles at me.

My Love I Know

She smiles through
day,
she smiles through
me,
but come my way
my love.

What makes the day
so blue my
love?

My love I know;
my love I care;
I know I love
you so.

Oh smile my
love;
oh rise my love;
don't give up soon
when the day is
young.

Why Stay So Long

How long my love?

How long?

The day seems dull,
the joy seems
gone,
as I wait and
wait for you my
love.

Why stay so long?

Why wait so long?

How I wish I
know the why.

I can see my river
flow away;
and my hope and
joy but seems
but gone.

Don't keep me here
too long my
love;
don't make me
wait my life
away.

Victor Akinrinmade

How Great The Day

For love,
for love,
I pray my dear;
I want you much
is the word to
say.

Don't make me
break her heart
my love;
as the dream and
song but makes the
deep, my love.

Oh my love,
my song,
my life;
how great the day
that makes my
day.

I've heard her talk,
I've heard her think,
but her dream but
comes my own.